STASH YOUR SWAG

100+ SECRET HIDING PLACES

TARRIN P. LUPO

Porcupine Publications

This book is published by Tarrin P. Lupo and Porcupine
Publications

FIRST Edition
ISBN 978-1-937311-22-3

DEDICATION

Leo Stedman, Ralph and Yolanda Lupo

I dedicate this book to both of my grandfathers. Each one in their own way taught me about the need to protect your valuables with stealth, not force.

Leo Stedman and Tarrin P. Lupo

CONTENTS

ACKNOWLEDGMENTS

Creative Editor and Typesetting:
Ruby N. Hilliard

Editor:
Sandie Britt

Illustrator and Cover Art:
Scott A. Motley

i

PREFACE

People have been hiding items since the beginning of mankind. Cavemen hid their food. Knights Templar hid their gold. Heck, even dogs and squirrels bury their food. Hiding places can be very simple, run of the mill, or incredibly complex, through force, threat, or thievery.

One of my grandfathers, who I called "Pop", taught me a very important lesson when I was a child that I will never forget. I once watched him disappear into his tool shed and come out with a handful of cash for shopping. I asked him, "Why do you hide your money; why not just use a bank?" He said, "I do use a bank for convenience, but I don't trust them and I always keep my real money at the house."

I was 10 years old and didn't know anything about banks. I had no idea what he was talking about. It was only years later that I fully understood. Questioning him, I asked, "Pop, why don't you trust the banks?"

He explained to me that before 1933, money was backed by gold and silver. During that time you could take bank notes from your wallet and cash it in for gold.

In 1934, President Roosevelt made it illegal to own gold or silver. The President did some fancy political maneuvering and passed the Gold Reserve Act. This, in turn, inflated gold from $20 to $35 an ounce. This increase would have made many Americans rich if they were allowed to keep their gold, but after confiscating it, the government owned it all. Overnight it became illegal to cash in paper notes for precious metals. From that point on, Federal Reserve notes were backed by absolutely nothing but a promise that those who did not recognize dollars as real money would go to jail.

I asked him, "How did the government force people to turn in their gold and silver for notes?" He went on and

ii

explained that they used banks as their muscle. Banks were assigned agents who would seize any metals they found and cash them out with Federal Reserve Notes at the lower $20 an ounce price.

Pop's father had a great collection of coins inside a safety deposit box. When he went to the bank to get them out, the bank forced him to open it under a government agent's supervision. When my great-grandfather complied, the agent seized the coin collection and gave him only face value for his precious coins. In other words, the agent treated the valuable coins as normal coins and not collectables that were worth 10 times the value.

Understandably, they never trusted banks again. Banks are quasi-government entities that will never protect you or your money. My grandfather only kept what he needed to pay bills in the bank. He would never trust his real valuables inside their walls again.

My Italian grandfather, the one on the far right in the picture below, also lost his fortune in the depression. (By the way, I am the angry baby in case you were wondering.)

When the stock market crashed, banks just closed their doors and all of my family's money was lost. As Italians, my grandparents knew not to trust the government or the banks. Italy's corrupt government is infamous. In that day, you kept your money close to you or close to your property. When my grandparents died, there were thousands of dollars hidden all over the house. It took over a year to uncover it all. I still doubt we found it all. Stacks of cash were hidden everywhere: in books, old newspapers, mattresses, furniture, secret rooms, and other random compartments.

So, could this happen today? Would a bank take your money? You bet they would! When the market crashed in 2008 and was dropping 500 points a day, there was a whole lot of chatter about closing banks and freezing accounts. The idea was to stop the market free-fall. This never happened, but just knowing that it was seriously on the table was enough for me to pull all of my assets out of their institutions.

Businesses' and individuals' money becomes frozen or is taken regularly. The government takes whatever they want, whenever they want, without having to explain why. They can legally hold your money during an investigation and unless you have years of free time and thousands of dollars to spare, you may have no hope of recovery.

So, if banks can't be trusted, what do you do? The answer is simple: hide your valuables really, really, REALLY well! It is crazy that we have to go back to hiding our swag just as it was during the depression, but the evidence is clear. The boogieman is real and he can take all your stuff now, without even a trial. Sure, there have always been mobsters and crooks, but now we also have to consider crooks in suits, too.

There are a whole lot of people who covet your possessions. They come in all shapes: government bureaucrats, lawsuits, opportunistic family members, pissed off ex-spouses, and, of course, robbers!

My philosophy is to minimize risk by spreading out money. Think of it like a hiding place mutual fund. You will want to put your money in many, many hiding places, so even if your house gets burglarized, the chances of them finding all the booty will be very remote.

You may also want to consider making a dummy bag. Fill big Ziploc bgas with costume jewelry and leave them throughout your pad, somewhere obvious. Some people take it a step further and use a dummy safe with a dummy bag. Leave the safe unlocked and a bad guy will think he got all your good stuff and leave quickly.

I have kept all my hiding places in this book doable under $50 so you can make many secret stashes. I encourage you to think of your own unique ideas or elaborate on mine.

Good Hunting,

Tarrin P. Lupo

STASH YOUR SWAG

100+ SECRET HIDING PLACES

TARRIN P. LUPO

Lupolit.com

1 CHAPTER

10 SECRET HIDING PLACES
IN THE YARD

#1
Using Hollow Trees and Fake Branches.

This is one of the oldest and most notorious hiding places made famous in the "Connecticut Charter Oak Incident." The Charter Oak was a huge tree originally planted in Hartford by a tribe of Indians as a symbol of peace. The settlers in 1630 refused to cut it down. During 1662, King James II loathed that colonies were making their own charters and ignoring his. In response, he sent an agent named Andros in 1687 to collect the American charters from the colonies and replace them with the king's version.

The legend goes that Andros demanded the Hartford charter from the colony and as the argument ensued, the candle that was lighting the room "mysteriously" went out. While it was dark, the charter was passed out a window to a man named Wadsworth. Wadsworth evaded the king's agent, ending the pursuit without the charter in hand. During the chase, Wadsworth had stashed it inside the hollowed oak. Andros searched everywhere, but to no avail. Eventually, he left frustrated and empty handed. Connecticut was so proud of their original act of governmental disobedience that they honored it by placing the famous oak tree on their state quarter.

For this hiding place to work, you will need trees. Find a hollow one with a good hole and insert your stash. You can also hollow out a thick dead branch. If you only have one tree in your yard, it will be obvious; this spot may not work for you. You will want to protect your valuables from the elements by placing them in multiple watertight plastic bags. The watertight bags can still allow in moisture, so you need many bags to completely water proof it. Also, if you are storing coins outdoors, don't let them touch the plastic bag directly. Over time, the plastic from the bag will turn the color of the coin and make it less valuable. Instead, wrap paper or cloth around them first.

#2
It's Raining Pennies!

The next hiding place was in the news a few years back and was surrounded by scandal. A couple of construction workers said they found a few hundred thousand dollars in a very old building while cleaning out a gutter. Later, the same construction workers were discovered to have been the actual thieves and had made the whole story up.

If you enjoy being creative, you should place your money in a watertight plastic container and then stick that into a completely sealed plastic bag. Wrap it at least 5 times. Take this little container, grab a ladder, and wedge it in your gutter. In this way, your package won't get washed away and water can still flow around it. People rarely look up and never think to look in there.

#3
Bury it Like a Pirate! Arrrg!

If you prefer your things at ground level, then you should choose a spot right alongside your house and bury your money one foot or so underground. Again, it is important to make sure your cash is in a container that will not be affected by moisture. Originally, people used to just bury their coins and booty. These days, people bury almost anything, including guns, ammo, and preserved food. Once you are done filling up the hole, place a decorative stone or statue over top of it to help you remember where you stashed your cash. X marks the spot. If you bury a metal container, be sure to place it near metal fence posts. If anyone searches with a metal detector, it will throw them off completely.

#4
Fake Birdhouse Roof

Placing a specially redesigned birdhouse in your yard is another great way to hide money. Just pull the roof off and install a ceiling. Then use aluminum screws to reattach the roof so it will be easy to get off later. All you have to do is place your money in a sealed container and place it inside the birdhouse. Secure it between the roof and the ceiling of the structure. This way your stuff is protected from birds and they can still have their home. Who would think of checking a bird house for money?! You can take it further and design it so the roof pops off easily and the stash will be hiding on the ceiling without disturbing the nest.

#5
Treasure Island and Nazi Gold

If you are lucky enough to have a pond in your yard, even if it is a little one, consider stacking rocks in the middle to make a small island. Hide your goods under something heavy so it doesn't blow over. Make it even better by placing a decorative object over it on the island. If you have a very waterproof vessel, you can sink it under the rocks.

If you have a large pond, you can sink large and heavy objects. One of the most famous examples of this was the story of Hitler's missing gold. During the last days of Hitler's regime, he had his gold sunk in nearby lakes. Each year since, a small bit of Nazi gold has been recovered in ponds near the bunker. Word of warning on this one: it is very easy for your cache to drift around in water. Make sure you weigh it down really well.

#6
Fake Plants

Since many people use fake plants throughout the yard, you can take advantage of that. Simply poke a hole in the soil and put your money in there. Cover it up and continue to let that faux plant distract with its beauty, all while it hides your hard earned swag. This can also be used in a home or office because fake plants are everywhere.

#7
Fake Sprinkler

You can use an old sprinkler head and hollow it out. It is simply much easier to find one already made. Just look it up on the Internet.

Sprinkler heads are great places to hide small stuff like keys or diamonds and gems. Be sure you stick it where it won't get hit with a mower.

#8
Fake Rocks!

Fake Rock

If you are really broke, you can break the bottom off a rock and hollow it out, but it is a pain. Again, it is much easier to just buy one already made. You can find one on the Internet for cheap. Just search "fake rock" or "rock safe" and you will find one.

#9
Fake Firewood and Logs.

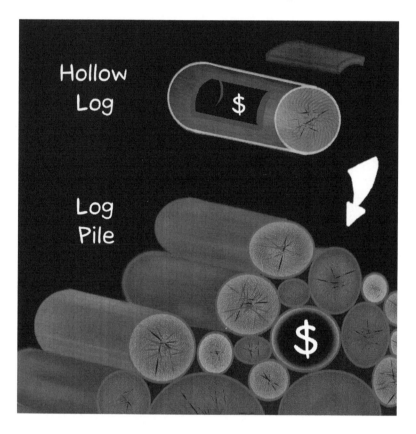

Many homes with wood-burning fireplaces have a stack of firewood in the yard. Now you can take the easy way and just hide a container in the stacks of wood, or you can make a hollowed log. If you have the tools, hollow one out and hide your stuff. This is great because you can get really large logs if you need a big storage space. A word of warning! Make sure you're the only one who brings in the firewood so nobody throws your safe on the fire!

#10
Satellite or Fence Posts

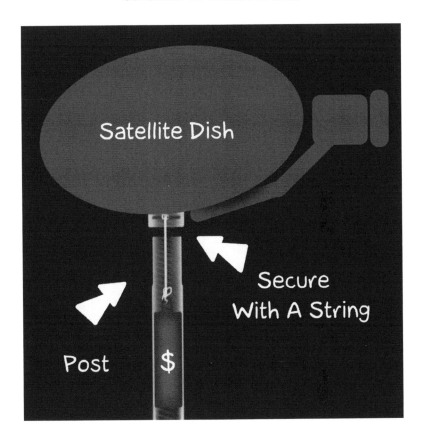

Some people do not attach their dishes to their roof. Instead, they simply put it on a pole in their yard. These poles are usually hollow and make a great place to drop stuff into. The difficulty is getting your stuff out. You will want to use fishing wire or very fine line that is hard to see. Tie it to your container and drop it down, then be sure to tie it to the dish. This can also be done with a hollowed fence post, too. Just take the cap off, drop it in, and use the cap to pinch the other end of the line when you put it back on the pole.

#10 ½ BONUS
Fake Power Box

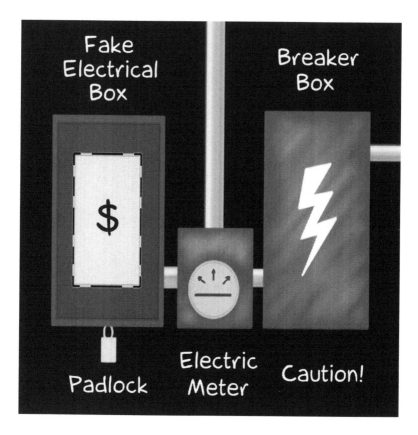

This is an old CIA trick. You can buy an old plastic power box and attach it to a fence, pole, shed, wall, etc...These are clean, large, and easy to attach. People tend to stay away from things marked high voltage. Workmen will never check it since they only service power boxes if they get a call that something is not working. Power workers never randomly open people's boxes. Since it is a fake box, I doubt they will get a call, but just to be sure, put your own lock on it.

2 CHAPTER

10 SECRET HIDING PLACES IN THE KITCHEN

If you are anything like me, you miss the days of unlocked doors and friendly neighbors. Unfortunately, we don't live in such a safe world anymore. Even though you might not be able to avoid a break-in that would keep your larger assets from being stolen, there are ways you can conceal smaller assets, especially in your very own kitchen. With a little preparation, one can keep a robber from finding things that reveal your identity. While the other items can be insured, your identity is something you can never get back!

#11
Ice Cold Papers

What my Pop always did with some of his important papers still works today. It was twofold genius; not only were these papers protected from robbers, but from fire as well. He always had a box in his freezer. It was a simple plastic container, and could easily be mistaken for leftovers. In this box were copies of birth certificates, mortgage paperwork, and bank info. Now, this box obviously couldn't contain everything that a file cabinet could contain, but you can put the really important stuff in there.

This of course can be used to hide anything. Just wrap your container in tin foil and mark it "steak 2005". Make sure you don't let anyone throw out your "spoiled meat"

#12
Cookie Jar

The kitchen cookie jar has always been the comically obvious place to hide things, but it still works. I used keep cookies in my jar, with a baggie underneath with money inside. This stops working when you get low on cookies, so a false bottom is a great idea. Try to find a similar material your jar is made of and fit it to the bottom.

#13
Silverware Drawers

For those who want to have a certain place to put paperwork, I always recommend keeping them under your silverware drawer. Not a very creative location for real important papers, but it is ideal for an easy and fast spot to access less important stuff or some quick cash.

#14
Now We're Cooking

Have you ever thought of placing them inside a cookbook on the shelf? Who is going to go flipping through a cookbook? This mainly works for cash. You can use this idea for any books, especially if you own a ton of novels. Another good idea is to use the cookbook shelf itself. Buy a thick board that you can cut into and make a hollow space.

#15
Rolling Paper

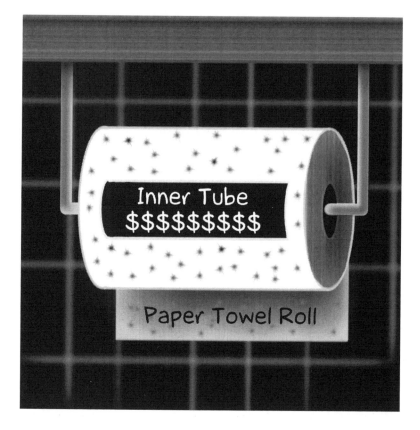

A smart place for short-term storage is in the hollow tube of a paper towel roll. Again, this might work better if you live alone. Be careful with this one; folks who don't know it is there could toss your stash. Also, weight is a factor; if you hide something heavy, like coins, the roll won't hold or spin right or it will fall down. In this case, lighter weight is better and rolled up cash works great.

#16
Dummy Appliances for Dummies

Find a crappy old mixer and pull out the inside gears, or if you're lucky, the stand is mostly hollow. Simply put it next to your blender, toaster, or any other appliance to camouflage it. Of course, any old, broken appliance will work, like a toaster, waffle maker, bread machine, or the base of a blender. You may still have a use for your old broken oven, fridge, microwave...etc. Why not recycle it and make it a hiding place?

#17
Pitchers and Bottles of Misdirection

A dark wine bottle, opaque container, or steel pitcher can provide a great place to sink your stuff. Simply get dark cola and drop it in your pitcher. This is a solid stash for short term hiding places. Now you do have to change out the cola every so often, but if you seal the pitcher well, it will last a surprisingly long time. You can use wine bottles, but not much fits in the opening and you might have to break it to get it out.

#18
Refrigerator Drainage Trays...GROSS!!

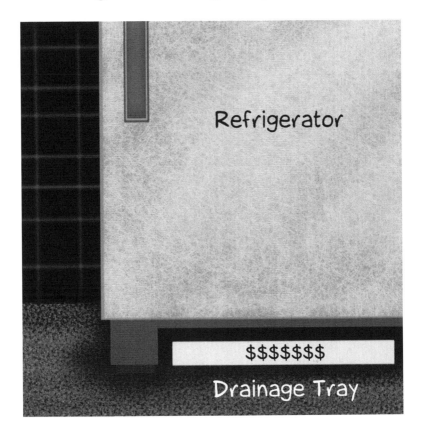

These trays live under your fridge and can be accessed easily. Now, they can get gross and moldy, so be sure to use a good watertight container. Also, this might not be a smart hiding place if your tray is overflowing with water all the time.

#19
Pans of Profit

Stacked Pots

$$$$

If you stack your pans concentrically, you will be able to stick cash between them. Try to put them between the sizes you rarely use. Try to find a pan you will never use with a big handle, and then hollow it out. Handles make great hiding places for small stuff. If you're lucky, you can find a cheap plastic spatula that already has a hollow handle with an easy to remove cap on the end.

#20
Boxes and Spices of Fortune

Boxes for flour, cereal, sugar, and spices can make fantastic hiding places in plain sight. Do not hide anything in a counter top canister of flour or sugar. Most burglars know that trick and will simply dump all of those canisters all over the floor. However, I have never heard of a thief who dumps out all the cereal and spices looking for booty. Just bag up your loot and drop it in the box or deep in your spice rack. If you have a ton of spices, put your bag inside one of the bottles. The possibilities are endless.

#20 ½ Bonus
Stuff your Meat

Carefully unwrap thawed meat, insert coins or other valuables, rewrap and freeze.

3 CHAPTER

10 SECRET HIDING PLACES IN YOUR BATHROOM

No matter the reason for wanting to hide your money, you have to make sure that you are hiding it well. Very few bad guys would look in a bathroom for hidden money so it could be the best place to hide your stash.

#21
Why is it so Cold in this Bathroom?

A faux heating vent can offer an alternative spot. Simply cut a hole in the wall and make a little box. Cover that box with a closed heating vent and no one will ever assume anything but hot air comes out of that vent. Do not hook it up and you never have to worry about fires. If your walls are deep, this is especially useful to hide large items.

#22
Sinkers and Floaters

This is an old favorite, but still works well if you make the water non-translucent. Take a roll of cash, put it inside of a tightly closed travel soapbox and add some weights. Place the soapbox in a plastic sandwich bag, just to be on the safe side, and hide it in the tank of your toilet. Someone would have to be a brave soul to look through your crapper in hopes of finding your hidden treasure. This works particularly well if you use the toilet cleaning bleachers that turn the water blue like 1000 Flushes. No one will be able to see the box under the water.

#24
Mirror, Mirror on the Wall

With a little time and the right tools, you can make your own safe behind a mirror or picture. You can get as detailed as you like, or simply put a small hole in the wall and cover it with the picture or mirror. With a little more effort you can remove the medicine cabinet and use the space behind it. The old styles have a big opening where they slide into the wall and they come off very easily.

#25
Tampon Boxes are Scary

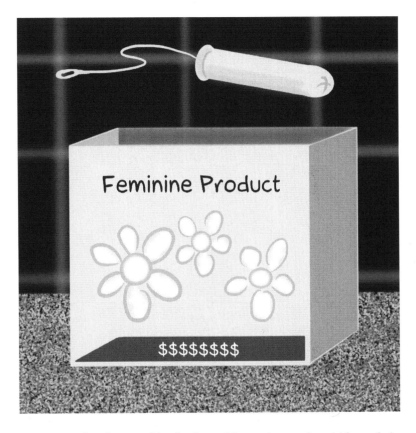

I got this idea from a friend who told me she used to hide cash in tampon boxes. I thought it was brilliant because most men are scared to death of feminine products.

#26
Fan Globes, Light Fixtures and Dead Bugs

Some light fixtures, such as the old globe style, have some room to hide small gems and diamonds in. They will look like dead bugs when lit up. Make it look authentic by throwing some dead bugs in there. You might think it looks untidy but at least you won't be poor and untidy.

#27
Sink Traps Save Marriages

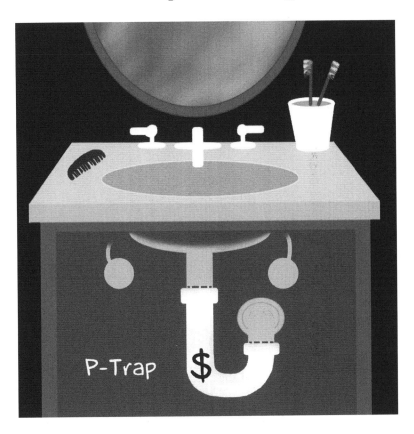

Most sinks have a "U" shaped pipe underneath called a trap. You probably know this if you have ever dropped your wedding ring down a sink. This is a great place to hide rings, but don't use traps for light objects. Please remember: only hide something that is heavy enough it won't wash away.

#28
Towel Rods of Treasure

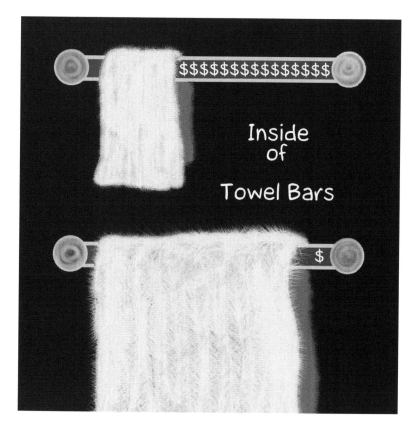

$$$$$$$$$$$$$$$$

Inside
of
Towel Bars

$

Some towel rods have a good diameter and come off easily. The best kinds are the spring loaded ones that come right off so you don't have to unscrew everything. You can stuff a small bag into the ends of these and put it back up in no time.

#29
Golden Shower

Inside
of
Shower
Curtain
Rod

The same applies for shower rods as towel bars, just make sure you water proof your bag very well before hiding it in the rod. Unfortunately, if you just have a bar or a dowel rod, you are out of luck on this.

#30
Stubbing Toes for Treasure

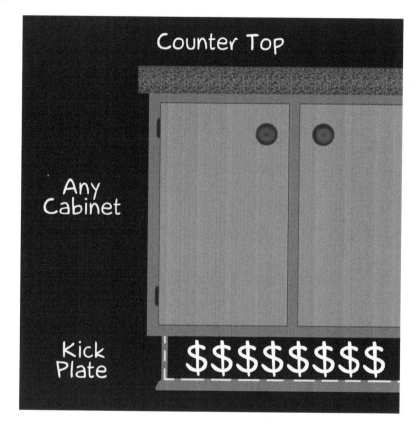

    Most cabinets and vanities have a small tow plate that is recessed and is against the floor. These can be taken off to reveal perfect hiding place behind them. This trick can also be done in the kitchen or anywhere with cabinets.

4 CHAPTER

10 SECRET HIDING PLACES
IN YOUR BEDROOM

We all lock our doors, make sure the windows are tight, and many have alarm systems. After all, prevention is the best remedy. No insurance plan can replace your heirloom jewelry or precious papers. Here are some ideas for hiding places in bedrooms. Did you know that when thieves go through homes, they often ignore the least used rooms? This makes a guest room the best choice for hiding treasures.

#31
Pillows of Deception

You can hide stuff easily in a quilt or pillow, but some folks take it further and place small safes inside them. You can actually disguise a small safe inside a pillow. This safe will blend in with actual furniture and bedding. It will sit in plain sight, and will often be overlooked by intruders. The pillow is an ordinary item that won't be mistaken as valuable so bad guys should ignore it. Pillows are my favorite choice, easy to open up and the padding makes your little safe hard to detect.

#32
Bed of Secrets and Lies

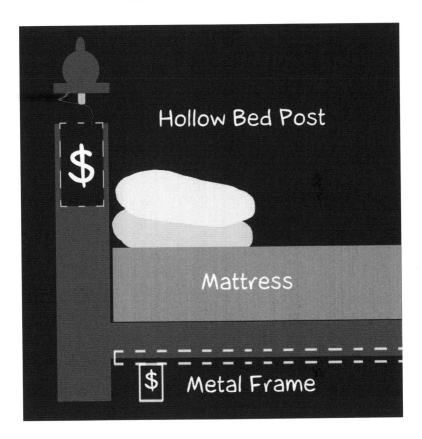

Use your bed, but not the traditional under-that-mattress spot. Take the time to unscrew the feet on your bed and drill holes into the posts large enough to insert your precious tokens. Reattaching the bedpost is really not difficult. This may be slightly time consuming on the front-end, but it is a really tricky hiding place. If you have a metal frame with plastic feet that fan out, it will be very easy to hide things in the space.

#33
Shelves of Stealth

Sometimes clutter is your best weapon for hiding stuff. If you have and old shop shelf like my grandfather did, it is easy to hide stuff in an old coffee can. Just throw screws and bolts over your prize and when a snoop opens the can, they will disregard any suspicion.

For certain items, you may want to tape valuables under a bookshelf. Simply remove the molding on the base, and use that inch or two to store your valuables. Then lock the molding back in place. If you don't want to remove the molding, check to see if it is open from the backside. An easier application of this theory is to flip a table or chair upside down and tape the valuables to the bottom of the seat.

#34
More Fun With Mirrors

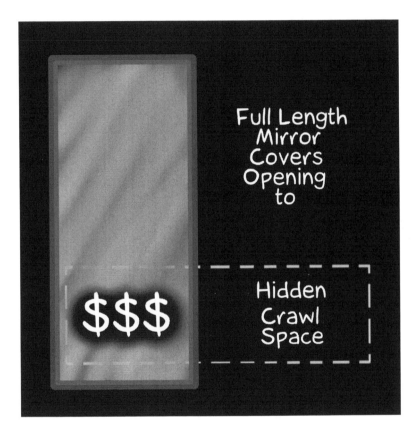

Mirror-Mirror on the wall…won't reveal your greatest secrets, not at all! Many full-length mirrors are hollow boxes. Put valuables inside the mirror, then conceal by replacing the plastic strip on the sides. Historically, full-length mirrors have been placed over secret doors and crawl spaces. Look around; do you have a small closet or crawl space? Is any entrance suitable to be hidden by a mirror?

#35
Base Boards and Slips

Need something more convenient? Use architectural secrets that your castle holds to squirrel away your nuts. Baseboards can be removed and the backspace hollowed, or you can cut a small hole into the drywall. When you put the board back it should cover the hole easily. The intelligence community refers to these spaces as slips.

#36
Door Slips and Fun with Jambs

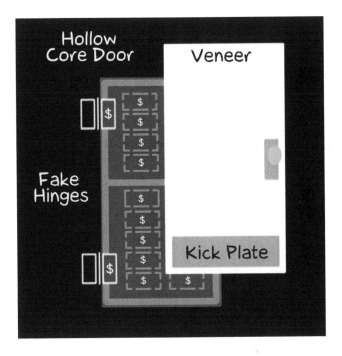

You can also dig out places on a solid wood door and use them as a slip, but the jamb is sneakier. Look for creative hiding spots within the frame, too. On a hollow door, the veneer on top comes off very simply with a good knife. Just glue it back on. A birdie once told me that a large, hollow door can hold up to $200,000 in hundred dollar bills.

One of my favorite tricks is to add a dummy hinge or strike plate. (What I mean by that is the plate on the doorjamb or frame where one side of the hinge connects) Just add an extra matching hinge to the door and hollow out a compartment behind the plate of the hinge that is on the frame. Since it is a dummy hinge, it just covers a hole in the doorframe. You can put one screw in to hold it down and still have plenty of room in your compartment.

#37
Hamper Hide and Seek

Two ways to enact this plan: make a fake bottom on the clothes hamper and keep some clothes over it or utilize the hampers that have a bag liner on the inside. Pull out the bag of clothes when you want to wash them. Just hide your stuff under the clothes bag against the floor of the hamper.

#38
Trashcans and Diaper Pails

You can use the same idea with a trashcan; hide your junk under the trash bag between the floor and the can. If you're real brave, use a diaper pail for the same idea. Most bad guys won't give the babies room a second glance, especially their soiled diapers. This is also a poor-man's shredder. If you don't have a shredder, then put sensitive papers inside the dirty diapers. Most identity thieves would never dive into a bag of used diapers.

#39
Fake Electric Socket or Dummy Plates

A very cheap way to hide stuff is to cut a small hole in the drywall and get a large dummy plate to attach over it. This works best around other sockets because it looks like it is supposed to be there. Be sure to be careful cutting into the wall and keep your hole shallow so as not to hit anything important.

For just a few bucks there is a dummy electric socket that is super easy to install. It is actually a safe with a key. You can get one if you just search for "socket safe" on the Internet.

#40
Fake Coin Safes

Fake Coin Safe

These days you can get much information on a very small SD card. If you have some sensitive pictures, information or files you want to keep private, try one of these cool coin safes. Make sure you hide it well s o someone does not mistake it for real money and spend it. You can find it on the Internet.

5 CHAPTER

10 SECRET HIDING PLACES IN YOUR ATTIC, FLOORS AND WALLS

These secret hiding places are throwbacks to the great depression. Take heed and listen to the old timers. My pop couldn't say it enough - "DO NOT TRUST BANKS!"

My Pop imparts financial wisdom to me at an early age.

#41
Gold in the Attic

You can hide most anything in the flooring of your attic. There is usually a small space for storage in your attic, giving you a chance to hide small valuables beneath floorboards.

Insulation can be a great hiding place. If the attic floor is wood, laminate, tile or even carpet, you can hide your valuables beneath it with just a little bit of work. If there is a floorboard that can be removed, create a box or container you can slip inside, then cover the loose board with a rug or mat to cover it up.

#42
Italian Secret Walls

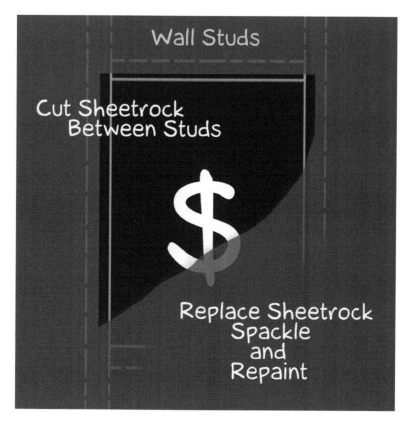

Hide your valuables inside your walls. Drywall is easy to cut open and replace. If you want to protect your stuff from being found for an extended period, storing them inside your walls may be a wise way to go. Drywall sheets are relatively inexpensive and you can easily spackle and paint a wall when finished. My grandfather made a small room inside a wall like this. It can be messy and time consuming, but an awesome way to hide stuff for a long time.

#43
A Picture is Worth a Thousand Dollars

Small items and stacks of cash can be hidden in the backs of picture frames. Not only can you use the art hanging on your walls, but if you store extra framed art in your attic, you can hide your valuables among them as well. Keep the modified picture frame in a big stack of other frames in storage and nobody will ever find it. A thief will not have the time and muscle to grab a stack of framed art up in an attic.

#44
More Ideas for Old Medicine Cabinets

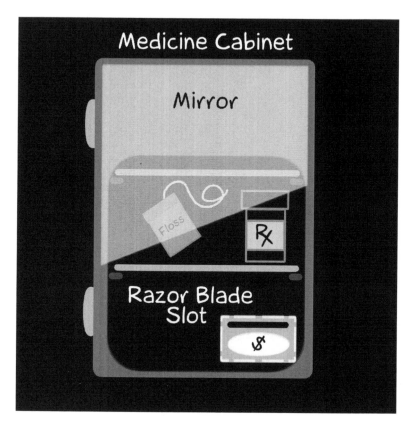

You can hide valuables in old medicine cabinets, which can be bought from auctions and flea markets. These old medicine cabinets frequently had slots in them that were used to dispose of used razor blades. Many people have used these slots to hide money and other small valuables. If you are looking for a quick and simple place to store coins or cash, turn an antique medicine cabinet into a trusty secret safe. Especially if it is sitting in a full attic of fixtures, thieves will just assume it is an old piece of junk.

#45
Golden Pipes

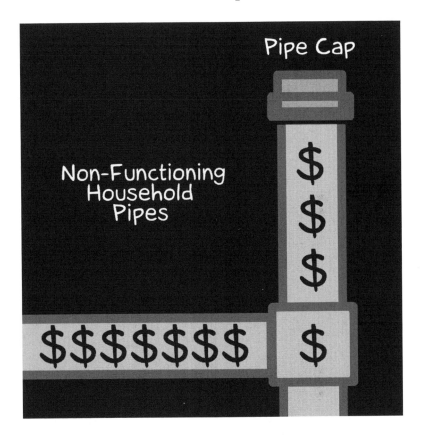

You can also hide select valuables in pipe safes, which most people have never thought of. There are many pipes in old homes that remain but are obsolete. In other words, there may be pipes in your old home that have no valves attached and are capped off. This provides an excellent place to hide valuables because they look like ordinary pipes; not many would assume that they hold precious inventory inside. Just make sure the pipe is detached from the water or gas supply and that there is no gas or water remaining in the line.

#46
Carpet Diving

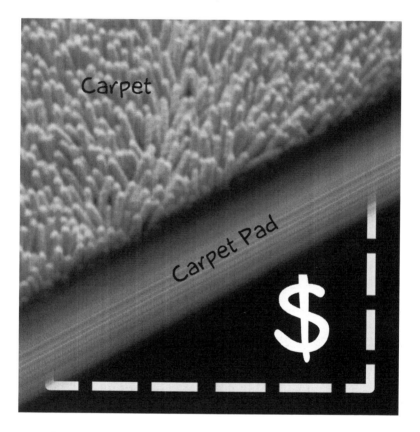

Carpet can be very easy to hide papers and thin objects. This also would work for decorative rugs, but the rugs need to be thick enough as to not show an outline of the stash. Most carpet has padding and that is why I prefer it. On a side note, I don't recommend you use something as obvious as a doormat for hiding a key to your house these days; everyone does that.

#47
Squeaky Floorboards and Tile

This trick is an old one that goes way back, but is still great, especially when used in old houses where there are loose floorboards and tiles. These can be wonderful hiding places for bigger objects, such as rifles or shotguns. Usually, there is more than enough room to hide stuff and the price is right!

#48
Blades of Fury and Fortune

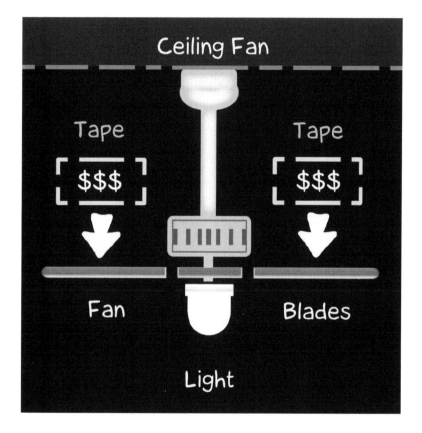

If you have a ceiling fan you never use, then this one is for you. Along the top of each one of your fan's blades you can tape your bills flat. Just make sure that you are lightly taping with painters tape, allowing you to remove cash later without ripping the money to shreds.

#49
The Rosenberg's Wall Trick

The Rosenberg's

The Rosenberg's were the most famous spy couple in American history. During the Red Scare in the 1950s, the government scared up and created paranoia so that everyone thought all their neighbors were communists. During this time, the Rosenberg's smuggled out sensitive files about the atomic bomb to Russia. The spy couple was caught and executed for espionage in 1953. Before he was executed, Julius uttered the famous quote, "We are the first victims of American Fascism."

The way they were rumored to have hidden the sensitive information was impressive. They hid it between the walls. They would get on a chair or ladder and push up the drop ceiling. The spies would look down at the space between two walls. If you don't know much about construction, think of the space where the insulation usually is these days. Back then, most interior walls had no insulation, so it was a big empty space.

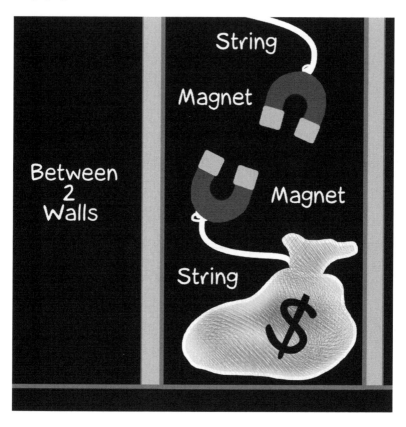

They would then put the documents in a bag, tie a string around the bag, and tie the other end of the string to a magnet. They would then drop the loot all the way down the inside of the wall. When they wanted to retrieve the documents, the spies would go fishing in the wall with a long string and a magnet. This is one of the best ways to hide stuff because someone would have to rip the walls out of your house to find your stash.

#50
The Crawlspace and Fake Junction Box

Most burglars would never spend time crawling under your crib while burglarizing. You really don't have to hide your valuables that well under the house; most people will never go in there. One of the best misdirection's is to use a dummy wire junction box or telephone box as a safe. If you want it to look convincing run some fake wires out of it. Don't forget to waterproof your stash well to protect it from mildew.

6 CHAPTER

10 SECRECT HIDING PLACES
IN YOUR CAR

Most of us have secret hiding places in our homes for our valuables. We have usually given this hiding place much thought and hopefully have chosen a place where a burglar would never look. Maybe we have invested in a wall safe and maybe we have been clever and used a food jar in the pantry. Well, what about when you need to hide something in your car?

Sometimes we cannot help it and must carry things that are of great value with us when we are traveling. This may be jewelry, coins, or even cash. Where are the best places to hide valuables in your car? The answer may be easier than you think.

Believe it or not, experts have found that the best hiding places are places that are very obvious and right under someone's nose.

#51
The Classic, Fix-a-Flat Can

One of the best hiding places is to use a pre-made hollowed out can safe that says Fix-A-Flat. You can find them by searching for the phrase "safe can fix" on the Internet. Make sure you sell this by putting it in a car emergency kit or car toolbox next to a can of oil and a wrench.

#52
Car Trash

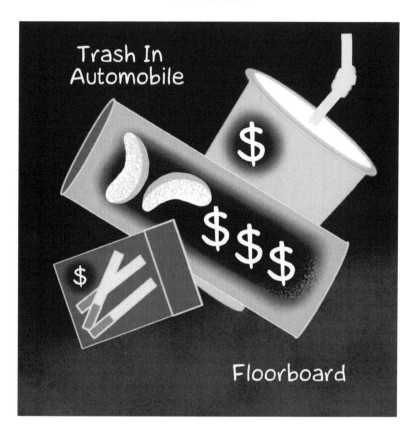

Sometimes clutter really helps you. If you're like me and have a messy car, it is easy to hide it in something like a Pringles can, or a bag of chips. Just take some chips out, put your stash in and then put the chips back on top. Those cans can last a long time, throw it in a pile of trash on the floorboard and nobody will give it a second glance.

#53
The Fake Seat Belt Buckle

The easiest way to make this work is to buy a seat belt extender used for obese people. You can open the buckle with a little work and hide something small in there.

The other ways can take a little more work to do, but it will be worth it. I rarely have people in my car and never use the backseat buckles. With a little amount of work, you can open the buckle and hide something small in there. If you do this, I would not trust this buckle again; just remember to take it out before you sell the car to someone.

If you need all your seat buckles, just go to a junkyard, buy a matching one, and simply attach a dummy one. Hide it in the crease of the seat. Unless someone is paying really good attention, it won't seem out of place.

#54
Car First-Aid Kit

Some newer cars come with built in first aid kits but if yours does not, just buy one and put it in your car. These are excellent places to stash your goods. They usually have bandages and little white plastic bags with various things in them. These little bags are opaque and a good size to hide small stuff in.

#56
Car Speaker

Car speakers come out pretty easy so people can upgrade them. Just use the empty space behind them to squirrel your treasure away.

#57
Back Seat Pocket

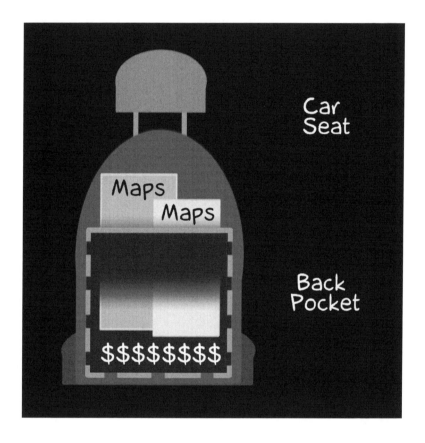

Most front seats have a pocket behind them that traditionally hold maps and papers. If you are hiding cash, you can slip them into the maps themselves, but for larger objects, use the bottom of the pockets. Throw some trash and clutter over your swag to misdirect anyone searching.

#58
Tire of Treasure

Inside Of Spare Tire

If you have a spare tire then this one is free. You need to take off the tire from the rim. I have been told you can fit $50,000 dollars in $100 dollar bills inside just one tire. Fill the spare with whatever you want and pop it back on the rim. This is a large place to store stuff, but cops do check this one sometimes.

#59
Ash Trays of Deception

A friend gave this one to me and since I don't smoke, I completely forgot about it. Ashtrays come out easily and are oftentimes overlooked. Simply hide your stash under the ashtray. It is fast and easy to get to.

#60
Broken Air Vents

Air vents come out easily. They have a space behind them where you can store stuff. Just make sure to keep the vent closed and try not to run the air too hot if you're hiding flammable cash.

7 CHAPTER

10 SECRET HIDING PLACES
IN YOUR TOOL SHED
&
MORE YARD IDEAS

When people come to your home in search of valuables, they will more than likely tear your home apart rather than search your yard or tool shed. So, if you are looking for secret places to hide your valuables in your tool shed, consider the following options which are low cost to free, and easy to implement

#61
The Other Black Gold

You can consider hiding your valuables in planters and flowerpots in your tool shed. While you may be able to hide small valuables on the bottoms of the flowerpots, another option is to hide things in or under the soil. This is especially useful if you are growing plants in pots, because most thieves are not going to break into your planters looking for keys and other valuables hidden among the roots and soil.

#62
Drawers, Coins and Keys

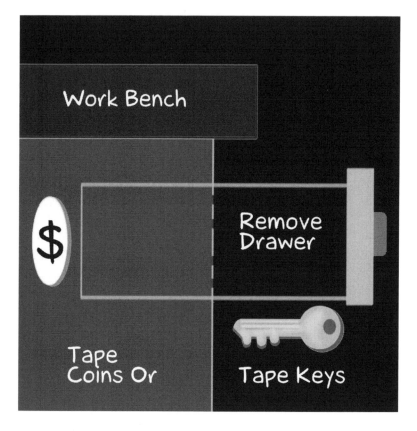

You may even want to consider hiding your valuables under the drawers in your workbenches and other furniture. Most people will rifle through the drawers without thinking to look beneath them. Small items like coins and keys can be taped to the bottoms or backs of drawers where they cannot be seen, and will rarely if ever be discovered.

#63
Be a tool, it's okay. Girls like it. Really!

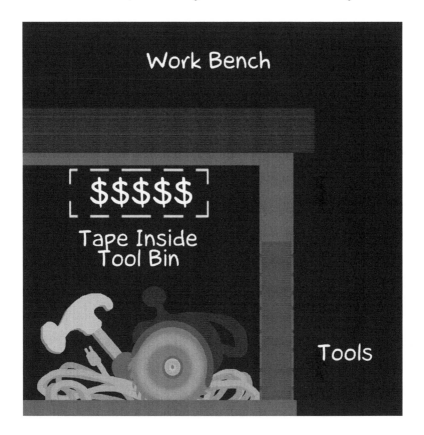

You can consider hiding your valuables with your tools. If you have many tools, there are bound to be interesting places to hide valuables in the mix. Some things can be hidden easily in toolboxes and tool clutter, allowing them to be hidden in plain sight. Hollowed handles in tools work great, too.

#64
Dirty Money

You may even want to consider hiding your valuables in bags of soil or fertilizer. You will want to wrap them in plastic and tape the packages to keep them safe and secure. Why not bury them in a bag of soil or fertilizer in the back of your tool shed? No one will want to rifle through a bag of manure or potting soil.

#65
Patio Furniture of Profit

Consider hiding your stuff in other places in the yard as well, such as inside the upholstery of patio furniture. Most patio furniture cushions and padding have zippers that allow you to remove the covers. This can backfire though, if bad guys are intent on stealing the patio chairs. Another plus to this idea: outdoor patio cushions are usually waterproof, thus preventing your goods from becoming saturated or ruined by rain or snow, etc.

#66
Bird Bath of Secrets

This is one of my favorite ideas. Just dump the water and lift the bathing dish completely off. You will be amazed by this quick and easy storage space. This one is a wonderful rouse.

#67
Decks of Dollars

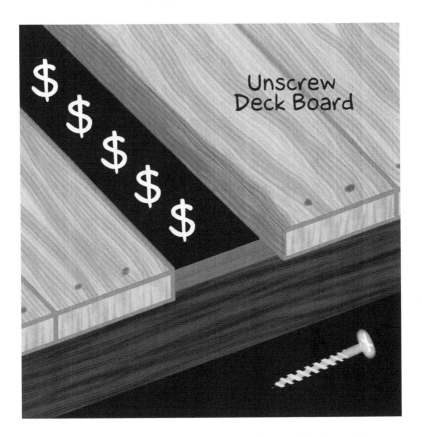

Decks can be easy places to hide stuff, depending on what the deck looks like. If you can crawl under it easily, then you can staple or nail a Ziploc bag full of goodies right to the underside of the deck. Also, this is a good place to bury your stash, too. If the deck is too low to the ground to get under, unscrew a decking plank and you have access to lots of storage space.

#68
BBQ Pit and Grills

Old Beat Up Grill

My grandfather built his own barbeque pit. Over time the pit had loose stones and bricks that made great hiding places. I know my friend never used his BBQ and would hide a key in his grill. This might not be a great idea if you use your grill a good bit.

#69
Timmy Fell in the Well

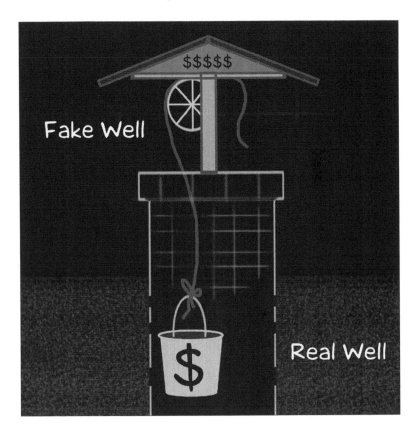

Real wells are hard to find, but many people have decorative wells. My Italian grandfather had two real wells and they made very good hiding places. The difficult part is fishing out the stash. Tie a line or rope to your stuff to ensure this process doesn't take too long. I prefer to keep it simple and hide stuff in the bricks or in the little roof over the well.

#70
Flower Bed of Mischief

This can be a wonderful place to bury treasure. Nobody will question why there is digging or fresh dirt in a flowerbed. You can also retrieve your stash with the guise that you are weeding your flowerbed.

8 CHAPTER

30 MORE MISCELLANEOUS IDEAS

Did you know there are many places to hide things to keep them safe from prying hands and eyes? A safe vault can be an expensive purchase, and it's the first place burglars look when searching for money, jewelry, or other valuables. Hiding things under a mattress is also another choice of many individuals and, in a burglary, is another popular place that thieves will check.

#71
Fake Backs

The false cabinet back is one of the best places for stashing money or other valuables. This can be a bathroom vanity or a kitchen cabinet. Have a piece of wood cut to the exact specifications of the interior cabinet dimensions. Choose the wood to match the backing of the cabinet or select another neutral color that is similar. Take some small pieces of 1x1 or 1x2 board to create the framework for your new, false backing. You can place your valuables in the small recess that is created and use a staple gun or small tacks to secure the false backing in place.

80

#72
Stair Drawers

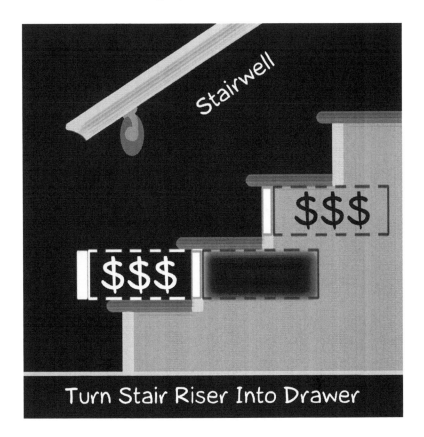

Turn Stair Riser Into Drawer

Now, if you made a whole set of these, it sure would get very expensive. If you do the work yourself and do just one stair, you can do it for under $50. This might take some work, but what a cool idea!

#73
My Little Tea Pot Short and Stout

Inside Tea Pot

If you are a collector of kitschy items such as inexpensive teapots and have many of these in a china closet, you have a readymade hiding place for some of your smaller goods. Should you only have a few teapots, this might not be your best choice for storing money or jewelry, as it would be more obvious, but if you have several dozen of these then using one could be a good idea.

#74
House Planet Safes

People often overlook the great hiding spot offered by a small, inexpensive pot that holds growing plants. Put your jewelry or money in a couple of waterproof plastic bags and place them in the bottom of the pot. Here your valuables can remain undisturbed and unseen, protected by the camouflage of potting soil and a green plant.

#75
Furniture of Loot

You can use a large sofa, chair, or ottoman as a safe if you take the time to cut a hole in the underside of the frame and place your valuables neatly into the opening. Make sure the hole you cut is not too big and secure the opening with super glue or sew it neatly back in place. This will protect your belongings even if the furniture is overturned or the cushions are searched. Burglars will not take the time or trouble to demolish a sofa or a chair inch-by-inch trying to find something that may or may not even be there.

#76
Cat's Love Shinny Things

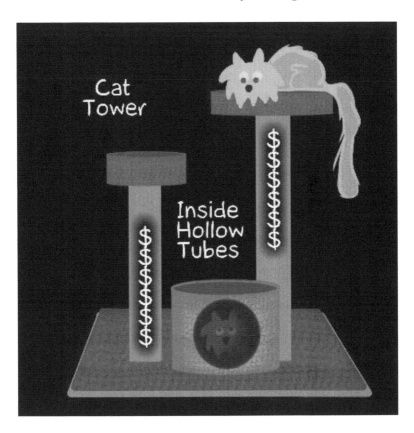

A cat condo has tons of places to hide stuff. Most have hollow PVC posts where you can stash your swag. Just tip it over and you will have access to the big tubes. Hiding your stash under the carpet in the little condos works great, too.

#77
Dirty Underwear and Skid Marks

Men's undies usually have a "pokey pocket" in the front. If you sew or glue one edge you have a little pocket. This works best with darker underwear. You can really keep people from checking them out by smearing some chocolate or fudge down the butt side.

#78
Is There Anything a Bra Can't Do?

This has already been a popular hiding spot for ladies for years, but the new bras allow new possibilities. I have been told this works best with gel filled or padded bras. Just pull out the falsies or padding and hide your stash in a pile of bras. Ladies, your secret is out, most men know you carry money in your bra anyway.

#79
Your Best Friend's Dirty Secrets

Inside Of
Child's
Toy

Little kids know this one really well. When I was a child I used to hide all sorts of stuff in the back of my teddy bear. This one is free and easy to do, just requires a little creative surgery.

#80
Beehive of Honey

I have been told some women hide junk in their hairdos. Of course I thought of the beehive immediately, but I am sure this would work with any big hair. Heck, this idea is worth its weight in gold if you live in New Jersey. Also, if you happen to have wigs around your house, you can hide all sorts of things in them as well as the Styrofoam heads that you set the wigs on.

#81
Bottom Heavy Lamps

Bases of lamps can be very useful. Try to buy one with a hollow base and just tape your stash in the hollow bottom.

#82
Crappy Old Electronics

Most burglars won't touch old electronics. If you have an old computer, TV, beta max, VHS, or boom box, gut it and use it as a cache. Chances are the thing does not work anyway, so why not repurpose it?

#83
Picking Pockets

A good place I used for years was shirts, pants, and coat pockets and it's completely free. Unless somebody has a whole lot of time to search 300 pockets, they are not going to mess with it. Just try to use a garment you never wear and make sure you don't donate it or sell it in a yard sale!!!

#84
Hollow Knowledge

Hollow books have been around for years, but they are still great. If you're a big reader and have a large library in your house, this spot is invaluable for expediency. The more books you can hide it in the better. Making a book safe can be a huge pain in the ass and much more difficult than it appears. It is so much easier to go the Internet and search the phrase "book safe." Also, if you do decide to make it, don't use the Bible or "Roberts Rules of Order." Those two books are way too obvious.

#85
I Love Looking at Other Peoples Cans

You can hide these in your kitchen, bathroom, or car. We covered the Fix-A-Flat earlier, but there are so many other great ones that look similar such as soup, sodas, shaving cream, etc. One of my favorites is a fake gas can. You can find all of these on the Internet and search using the phrase "can safe."

#86
Man's Best Partner in Crime

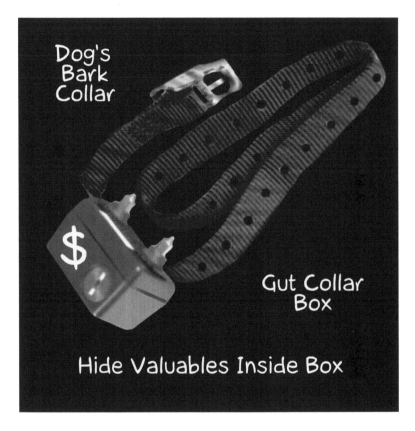

I had a dog that had the shrillest and most annoying bark on earth. It would make your spine shake when he barked. It got so bad I got a bark collar to train him to stop. Guess what? All it did was piss him off and make him bark more. So I hollowed out the thing and it was a great place to hide small things like a key. The dog doesn't even have to wear it; just leave it with all your dog stuff.

#87
Dog Bed and Toys

Almost all dog beds have a removeable exterior cover with lots of different places to easily hide stuff inside. My dog also loves these plastic cubes and toys. One side of them unscrews and you can fill it with kibble, then when the dog rolls it around, food comes out. The hollow space gives you a lot of room to hide objects. This one is easy to use. Any dog or cat toy will work great, but be very careful never to use a toy your pet really likes. Otherwise your cash will get shredded and buried in the yard.

#88
Hollow Heels

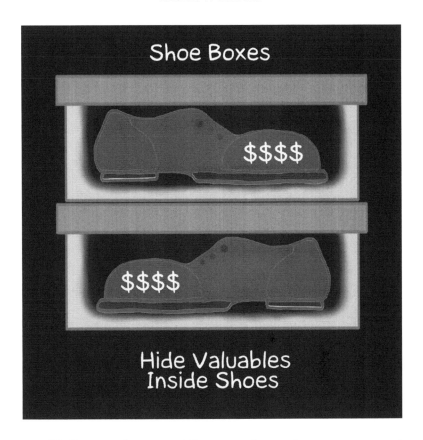

Unfortunately, some idiot on a plane who was crazy and tried to light his shoe on fire ruined this one for travel. It still works in your house though, especially if you own many shoes. You can simply hide your stash in the shoebox or stuff it in the shoe itself. An even better way is to use one with a thick sole with a section cut out.

#89
Peg Leg

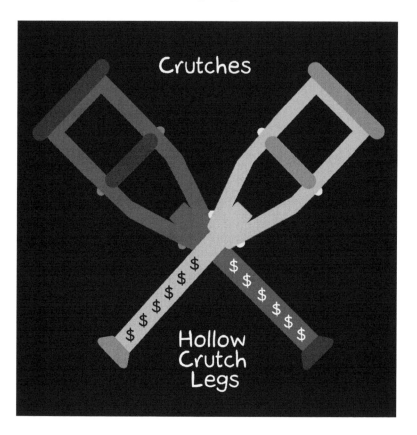

    I had heard a story of a smuggler who was an amputee. He would hide his stash in a fake leg. Few of us have missing appendages, but if you want to hide your valuables on yourself while you travel you can use a cast, sling, wheelchair, or crutch.

#90
Wacky Water Filter

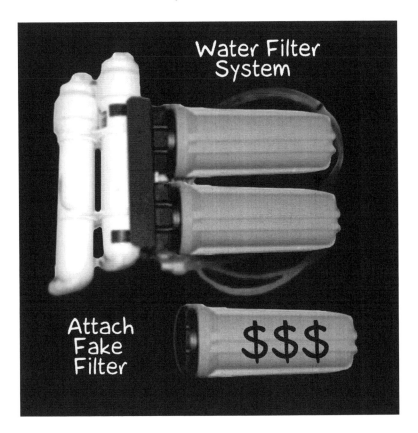

We have an under the counter water filter, but I don't see why this would not work on a regular pitcher style water filter, too. This would even work on the larger home water filters if you were clever enough to rig it. You don't want to mess with the water flow and the real filter. Just attach the hollow dummy filter case next to the others and it will fit right in with the real ones.

#91
Bambi Looks Like He is Hiding Something

My friend Ron gave me this one. Most hunting households have a deer head on the wall. The deerskin is sitting on a hollowed out tube. You can cut into the backside or some models let you pop the head right off the mounting board. Why not let Bambi keep your secrets?

#92
Fluffy Jackets and Puffy Shirts

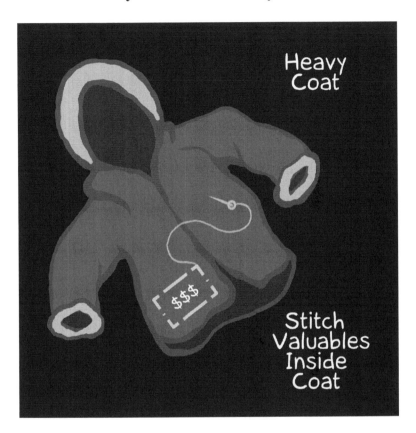

One of the best ways to move large amount of cash and papers is to sew it into a puffy jacket. This is the method the famous card counting team from MIT used to move large amounts of cash safely. They made a special leather jacket that could hold almost $30,000 dollars to sneak through the airports with. This idea makes a great hiding place and works really well if you have a ski jacket.

#93
Time is Money

A grandfather clock is another way to hide things. You don't really want to go up into the clock because they are very easily damaged and VERY expensive to fix. Instead, go to the very bottom and drop your stash in there and it will be easy to access quickly.

#94
Secrets in the Window

The windowsill has a hollow space under it. On some windows there is molding you have to take off first. There is a space that can be used for long term storage needs. This is time consuming, however, and may not be best for fast access to items.

#95
Sleeping with Guns

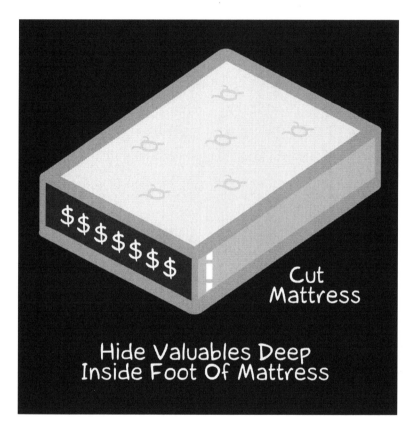

I know when you think of hiding stuff under your mattress you think that has been played out. I agree; most burglars just throw the mattress on the floor and it exposes everything under it. I would like to use the mattress for another idea. I know a guy who cut into his mattress at the foot of the bed and would hide his rifles in there. If you cut the mattress and hide things deep inside, it is works great. Just duct tape or sew it up. I also recommend the foot of the bed so you won't feel a gun in your back while you sleep.

#96
Santa's Treasures

You can hide your cache on the outside of the house in loose bricks on a chimney. A better idea is to stick the stash on the inside of the flue. Let's face it, if you are a regular fireplace user, this will not be the best spot for you. If you have a non-functional fireplace, this is a great idea.

#97
Statues and Pedestals

Most statues and pedestals are not solid. They usually have a hollow bottom that you can easily access at a moments notice.

#98
Speakers of Surprise

Inside Of A Large Speaker

    Speakers are easy to open up and have lots of extra room. My friend Jason gave a twist on this idea to me. He said, "In college, I had a gigantic subwoofer that took up the entire closet. We used to put kegs in there." I think it is a great way to hide large objects like a keg, or a gun. Kudos Jason!

#99
Stove Hoods and Fan Housing

This one can be fun if you're handy. Most hoods have a filter that drops right out and has a hiding place behind it. Don't be dumb and put paper or cash in there or you will have a nice fire. Use this for coins and such that won't be affected by heat. Also, do not block the entire vent; that could cause your fan motor to overheat.

#99 1/2
Fake Bottoms

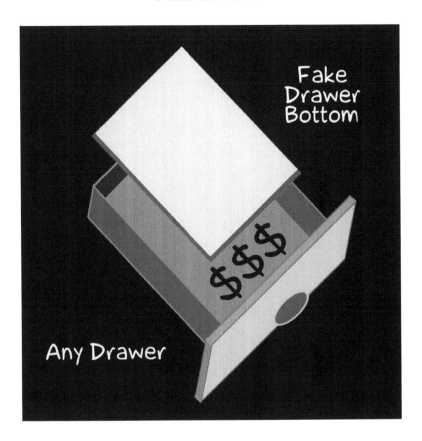

We have addressed fake backs in drawers, but I forgot to mention fake bottoms. This will distract thieves from thumbing through prized possessions. Simply cut a thin piece of wood to fit on bottom. Cover the new board with paper and you would never know it is there. You should be able to hide cash or papers easily in the thin space.

#100
The Ultimate Hiding Place

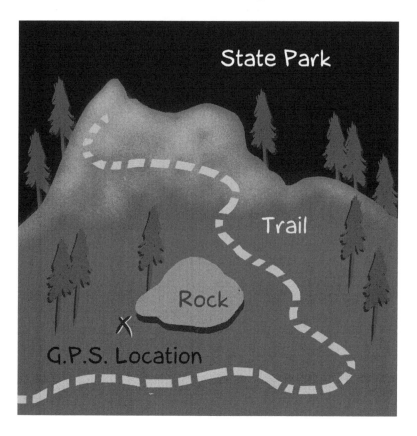

If you want to hide large quantities of things, there is a famous spy technique that makes it impossible to find. Burying your booty is the best way to hide it, but the problem is where to bury it. If you hide it on your own land, there is a good chance that eventually someone with enough patience can find it. This also goes for all other lands you are associated with, like rentals, family land, even your friends. You never know when some worker may begin digging or if the land gets developed without you knowing.

The way to avoid all of this is to find a large state park that you know will never be developed. Hike in a few miles and go off path for a while. Pick a good private spot and dig.

Some warnings: Don't use your own computer to search for a park and map it. Don't bring your phone with GPS. Don't bring anything but an OLD GPS unit and a camera. You want an old one that does not track you like a phone does. Buy a used older GPS out of the paper, so it is not identified with you in anyway. When you get to your dig location, turn on the GPS and memorize the coordinates. Take some pictures so you know the exact location.

Destroy the GPS or get ride of it so it does not get back to you. Of course, if you are amazing with a compass, you can do that, too, if you don't want to bother with a GPS. Another great way to avoid traces back to you is if you know of a special place in the park that is private and you know how to get to that location without directions.

If someone finds the pictures, they will have no clue where they were taken. The coordinates are now forever in your brain. If you want, write them down in a code only you would know and bury it somewhere easy to find.

That might seem extreme, but if you really have to make something disappear, it does not get better than that.

It is my greatest hope that with all of these ideas you will find ten that you can easily implement. A combination of many hiding places is always recommended. Don't keep everything in one stash.

One last word of advice: it is important to leave a video or a written list of all your hiding places with someone you can trust. Otherwise, if you get sick, incapacitated, or die, no one will be able to find your stash. I am reminded of the famous saying, "You can trust two people if one of them is dead." It is a wise saying and a warning; be very careful to whom you leave the list. The best way is to hide the it is in one of your best caches and just tell one trustworthy ally about that place. Then, if you stop trusting that person, you just remove the one list and hide it somewhere else.

I hope this book does not make you too paranoid, however, THEY are always watching!!!

Thanks for buying *Stash Your Swag*. Check out my other books on Amazon or at www.Lupolit.com!

ABOUT THE AUTHOR

Tarrin P. Lupo is a full time author and liberty activist. Some of his other books include the *Pirates of Savannah: Birth of Freedom in the Lowcountry* trilogy, *Stash Your Swag,* and *Catch that Collie.* He enjoys rugby, chess and cuddling with his cats and dogs.

15318602R00074

Made in the USA
San Bernardino, CA
21 September 2014